Learning Forgiveness

By Aaron Fields

CONTENTS

Something To Think About Before You Read

"In life, you can't expect others to have compassion towards you if you're not willing to have some level of compassion towards them"

----------Aaron Fields

When was the last time you said "I forgive you"?

Word From The Author

The reason why I am touching on this subject of forgiveness is because forgiveness seems to be a major problem to cultivate. What does having a peaceful mind mean to you? How do you envision peace in your own life? Whatever it is that you're imagining right now as it pertains to peace, it should be similar to how you embrace forgiveness. None of us are perfect, but it's time to stop feeling angry, resentful, and bitter.

When you decide to forgive and move on with your life, you're more so doing yourself a favor, not the person that wronged you. When was the last time you got angry at someone? Are you still holding a grudge? Are you struggling to move on? Keep in mind that you are the one in charge of holding the grudge not them. Don't allow yourself to be locked into a mental cage because it will prevent you from moving on. The last thing you want is increased stress and a decreased level of empathy towards other people in your life.

Always remember that not only forgiveness is an ongoing process, but forgiveness is going to look different for everyone. It ultimately comes down to you being confident and firm in your decision that you are willing to move on with your life by getting rid of all the anger and resentment. Forgiving someone does not necessarily mean things have to go back the way they were or you have to invite that person back into your life. Sometimes depending on how bad the situation was, certain things may never be the same again, and that's fine. You'll be surprised at how your mind starts to become uncluttered once you start to move forward in life.

Why is Forgiveness an Issue?

The reason forgiveness can be a major issue in certain communities is because the individuals can't seem to create a code of ethics or operate based on a common method. Now there are some people that know how to operate on a higher level than most when it comes to forgiveness and integrity. However, because most people can't or don't want to understand how other people live their lives and how they make certain decisions, we don't cut them any slack. Let's be honest, most of us if not all of us have issues with forgiveness depending on the situation and the individual we're dealing with.

Whether it was a family member, a close friend, or even your spouse that did you wrong, learn how to move forward with your life. It's not healthy to hold in anger and resentment. It's not healthy to dwell in the past, especially if you're trying to move forward. When you're fixated on negative energy, life will not only affect your future, but your perspective on life. What do I mean by that? In life, when we continue to dwell on our negative experiences, life will prevent us from excelling, mobilizing, and reaching high levels of success. Believe it or not, there are some individuals who are still bitter about the things that happened to them thirty years ago from someone who might not even know that they still exist anymore, or it might be possible that they completely forgot about the situation. Either way, the point that I'm trying to make to you is that at some point, you must move on with your life. You don't want to end up living a life filled with bitterness, anger and resentment.

Do you think having issues with forgiveness can correlate with loyalty? The reason I ask this question is that in most cases the more loyal a person is, the higher the expectations they have on others. It's important to understand that when someone doesn't show the same level of loyalty that was instilled in you, you might develop a lot of resentment towards that person. If you're not careful and you continue to build more resentment, you'll end up developing a cynical attitude towards anyone you encounter. Don't allow your negative experiences to get to a point when you shut yourself off from the world. Yes, there are people who will take you for granted and mistreat you, but when you distance yourself from everybody, you will prevent yourself from displaying your gifts to the world. That's why it's important to forgive others and move on, because if you can't forgive other people, how do you expect the world to forgive you?

What Is Forgiveness?

I understand that forgiving others can be extremely difficult. Like I mentioned earlier in the previous chapter, when you're a loyal, faithful, and dependable person, you'll assume everybody else exudes those same traits. Everyone is different and if you continue to have high expectations for everyone, you'll be disappointed repeatedly until you realize that not everyone is like you.

There are various ways to define forgiveness. If you ask me, I believe forgiveness doesn't mean that everything has to go back the way things were before that person wronged you. Depending on how bad the situation was, you probably don't want to have anything to do with that person anymore. Regardless of the situation, you must have the ability to move forward because there will be times in life when you offend and hurt people as well. Can people forgive? Yes, but at the same time it is hard to forget.

Listen, we've all been victimized by someone and we've all mistreated someone in some shape or form. What makes forgiveness so important is going to be based on the level of sincere and authenticity. No matter the outcome, always keep in the back of your mind that you are going to move on with your life.

Doing Favors

When you encounter different people in your lifetime, it's possible that you are going to do someone a favor. Understand that we as individuals have an investment on the people we choose to help. If you come across a person who wants to help you, not only you should thank them, thank God as well. Why? Well, from a biblical standpoint, God is our head, and that's who we should all try to model ourselves after the best way we can. Now are we all going to fall short of God's standards? Yes, because we are human beings, but at least if we continue to have that motivation to be like God, we'll be able to improve and solve most of the issues we have within ourselves and in our community.

When you decide to help someone out that's dealing with a lot of hardships in their life and they're still unappreciative, never get angry or upset with them. You know why? It's because when you help someone, you should do it out of the kindness of your heart. Many times in life we get frustrated with certain people because they didn't appreciate the favors we did for them. Let me ask you this, why do you get upset when people are not thankful for the things you did for them? Is it because you weren't doing it out of the purity of your own heart? Is it because you want recognition? Is it because you're seeking validation? Or is it because you want something in return?

Let's be honest, most of the things we do for others have an incentive. Believe it or not, very few people in society do things for other people without asking for something in return. I encourage you to get in the habit of doing certain things for others while expecting nothing in return (if that's truly what your heart desires). When you do things out of the kindness of your heart, the reward you get in return will be far much greater.

Most people in life expect something in return after doing someone a favor. Does this apply to you or to someone you know? If so, has there ever been a time when someone didn't appreciate you after what you did for them? Did you become bitter? Or did it not bother you? Give me your thoughts.

_____

_____

_____

_____

_____

_____

_____

_____

_____

_____

_____

_____

_____

_____

_____

_____

_____

_____

Predestination

When a person mistreats you, always conduct yourself in a mature manner so that way the person who treated you unfairly will receive the appropriate retaliation. What do I mean by that? When a person mistreats you, don't seek vengeance and retribution. When you seek revenge on someone, you're preventing that person from receiving their punishment. Please understand that what goes around comes around. When a person mishandles or abuses you, they are going to get what's coming to them at some point down the line because it's predestined. More importantly, your hands will be clean, because you decided to not take matters into your own hands. Sometimes in life you just have to not take any action and just let God handle it.

Forgiveness does not mean you should just forget about it and act like nothing happened. When it comes to these situations, you must always remind yourself to operate on a higher level. One of the major obstacles that stop individuals from operating on a higher level is their relationships. Unfortunately, many people hold on to certain indignities that were done to them in the past, but you must understand that this is a dysfunctional society we're living in. Just because this world is already chaotic, doesn't mean you have to be chaotic as well. When you find yourself constantly getting hurt in these relationships, don't waste your time by going back and forth with the other person because it never leads to anything productive. Let them go and stop contemplating on how you're going to settle the score. If you indeed were the victim in the situation and you're the person who was in the right, forgive them, let God take care of it, and let them go so they can fall into their next situation. Whatever happens to them after that is predestined, so if I were you, I'd move on with my life.

5

Forgive Yourself

In life, sometimes it's easy to forgive others, but how often do you forgive yourself? A big important aspect to forgiveness is learning how to forgive ourselves. Many people are traumatized and have dealt with a lot of pain and suffering in their experiences. There are people who were abandoned, women who may have been raped or sexually assaulted. There are some individuals who were molested as a child, young men that have been locked up and forced to live and embrace a toxic environment, etc. Because of these experiences, the individual takes it out on themselves by using drugs, alcohol, or they might even attempt suicide.

Forgiving yourself is a major component to surviving in this world. I'm sure there is someone you know in your personal life that constantly has to be reminded of their personal achievements as opposed to the trials and tribulations of their life. The reason they act this way is because they have trouble forgiving themselves for certain things that weren't even their fault. If this applies to you, don't be so hard on yourself over the things you can't control. Whatever you had to endure in your life, I hope and pray that you come out of the situation a better human being, but please understand that not everything in life is your fault.

No one is perfect and everyone makes mistakes, but learning how to forgive yourself is essential to your mental health. Forgiving yourself means that you accept what has happened, not condone it. Whatever transpired in your life, move on from it without ruminating over your experiences.

Have you ever had trouble forgiving yourself? If so, what was it that transpired in your life that was causing you to dwell in the past? Are you still not over that stressful event? Or are you in the process of learning how to move forward with your life?

_____

_____

_____

_____

_____

_____

_____

_____

_____

_____

_____

_____

_____

_____

6

Don't Lose Sleep

Have you ever lost sleep before? Many of us have had a hard time getting sleep because we still think about the person who wronged us. When you interact with a friend, family member, significant other, or even a random person, always try to take the high road. Why? It's because many times when you're dealing with certain people that are disrespectful and not loyal, they'll try to cover it up by acting nice. When a person is acting nice (operative word acting), and they have a hidden agenda to sabotage you, remove yourself from them. As a matter of fact, refrain from even responding to them and let them float off into their future life, whatever that may be.

The reason most people act nice towards other people even though the victimizer understands that they're doing something they shouldn't be doing is to absolve themselves of being a troublemaker. In other words, you'll encounter a lot of your enemies that will try to act like they're the victim. When you encounter these types of people in your lifetime, move on and don't lose sleep over them. Understand that if you decide to go back and forth or engage in an argumentation with these kinds of people, it will validate their claim that they are the victim rather than the predator. Eventually it's going to make them think that they're not doing anything wrong. As a result, the victimizer or predator starts to think that they can get away with anything, which is why you need to ignore them while making sure that your mind is focused on higher things. While you're here on this earth, I encourage you to develop a strong and spiritual connection with God. I also encourage you to accumulate knowledge and always seek wisdom. Your best friend should always be yourself first. Is it great to have friends? Is it great to have a powerful family? Yes it is, but your best friend has to be you first because you have to be the one to look out for yourself. Most people don't understand that your peace of mind has to be a priority over everything else.

Dwelling on your negative experiences not only affects your quality of sleep, but it will also negatively affect your quality of life. Holding on to old issues can take years off of your life. Is it going to be hard to forget certain things? Yes it will, but you must occupy your mind on things that are positive and fruitful. With that being said, what are your thoughts on dwelling over the negative things in your life? Have you ever lost sleep over something, or someone? What are some things you can do to be more constructive with your life?

_____

_____

_____

_____

_____

_____

_____

_____

_____

_____

_____

_____

_____

_____

_____

_____

Final Message

Always remember that forgiveness is going to be an ongoing process in your life. When you develop connections with people, keep in mind that every person is going to be gone one day. You must accept and come to terms with the fact that all of us will not be here forever. It doesn't matter who it is; it doesn't matter how much you mean to them, and it doesn't matter how much you love them. One day your parents are going to pass away, one day your siblings, friends, spouse, and your children are going to pass away. Hopefully, you'll be fortunate to live a very long and fulfilling life with the people close to you.

Please understand that it's important to prepare yourself and make yourself comfortable for the difficult transitions that are going to take place in your life because if you don't you'll self-destruct. As it pertains to forgiveness, if you can't accept the fact that other people are not going to operate on the same level of respect and loyalty as you do, you will self-destruct. That's why you shouldn't take certain people more seriously than they take themselves. In general, you really shouldn't take everyone too seriously anyway because doing that makes it easier for people to destroy your peace of mind.

If you expect other people to forgive you, you must be able to forgive others because one day you're going to be held accountable for all the things you've done in your life. As it pertains to forgiveness, I'm not saying you should pretend nothing happened and I'm not saying you should go back to being best friends with that person, but you have to move on. Just because someone screwed you over twenty years ago, doesn't mean you have to go out of your way to tarnish their reputation, or try to set them up to get killed.

Once again, you don't know how much time other people have on this earth with you. One of the most regretful things you can do in this world is to end things on an unpleasant note with someone, especially if you knew you had a chance to patch things up with them. Forgiveness is important to your healing process, and it's going to help you let go of all the anger, bitterness, resentment, shame, sadness, and guilt in your heart. The sooner you're able to understand that making mistakes is inevitable and certain people in this world will mistreat you, the more prepared you'll be when life throws you a curveball.

ABOUT THE AUTHOR

Aaron Fields is the founder and owner of The Write Perspective, LLC. He gives great advice to children and adults on how to enlarge their freedom and opportunities by helping them change and improve certain aspects of their personal, professional, and spiritual lives. Aaron Fields graduated from the University of Texas at Dallas with a bachelor of science in Speech Language Pathology & Child Development and a master's degree in Human Development and Early Childhood Disorder.

The purpose of The Write Perspective is to serve the personal, social, &/or spiritual development needs of individuals who have the desire to learn, grow, and develop the right perspective. Aaron Fields resides in the state of Texas where he continues to write his books and blogs with the explicit intention of helping his readers and audience to change or improve some aspects of their personal, professional and spiritual lives. Aaron Fields travels to 50+ cities a year in the United States and abroad to help others understand their identity, create their purpose and how to utilize their gifts and talents for the betterment of humanity. During his travels, Aaron Fields inspires and mobilizes in early childhood centers, schools, colleges, juvenile facilities, prison, churches, and community neighborhoods. In addition to his books and public events, Aaron Fields spends a great portion of his time improving the health and well-being of young children as an Early Childhood Consultant because he believes in unlocking the true potential of the youth.

STAYING CONNECTED

Share Your Story

Email me at **authoraaronfields@gmail.com** and share your thoughts about this book. Feel free to also share your story and personal breakthrough. Let me know how **_Learning Forgiveness_** has affected your life.

Allow Me to Partner With You

Need a mentor/life coach? I'm ready to walk with you through the process. Email me at **authoraaronfields@gmail.com** or visit twperspective.com, select life/spiritual coach and book your session today!

Need a Speaker?

Are you looking for a dynamic speaker for an upcoming conference, organizational training event, or workshop? Visit twperspective.com

Follow Me

twperspective.com – visit me here to order additional copies of **_Learning Forgiveness_** and gain insight into all of the resources The Write Perspective offers individuals and organizations.

Instagram: _twperspective

Twitter: @_TWPerspective

Linked In: https//www.linkedin.com/in/aaron-fields-022092104

Notes

Forgiveness Activities:

What exactly is holding you back from moving on with your life? Describe your thoughts and past events associated with your negative thinking. What was said or done to you, specifically?

_____

_____

_____

_____

_____

_____

_____

_____

_____

_____

_____

_____

_____

_____

_____

_____

_____

_____

_____

_____

Who is responsible for hurting you? Describe the past event and where the accountability lies. Is it the other person's fault? Or is it your fault? What role did you play in the situation?

_____

_____

_____

_____

_____

_____

_____

_____

_____

_____

_____

_____

_____

_____

_____

_____

_____

_____

_____

_____

How do you plan on taking ownership of the situation and the consequences? Keep in mind; you must accept the fact that you have to learn how to deal with the outcomes and the way how you feel from here on out now lies in your hands.

_____

_____

_____

_____

_____

_____

_____

_____

_____

_____

_____

_____

_____

_____

_____

_____

_____

_____

CPSIA information can be obtained
at www.ICGtesting.com
Printed in the USA
BVHW020847091222
653829BV00008B/23

9 781953 962119